# Damn Good Paleo

## So Easy - Anyone can do it:  Everyday Mouth Watering Breakfast, Lunch, Dinner and Dessert Recipes

# Summary

This guide is dedicated to providing people with information on all sorts of different recipes that can be utilized while on the Paleo diet. This is a popular diet that entails the body using foods that were similar to what people would have eaten in the Paleolithic Era. The foods are designed to where they will be made with safe and easy to use ingredients that don't contain dairy or harsh additives.

The book includes sections for breakfast, lunch and dinner as well as dessert. There are a few appetizers to include in this book as well. Each recipe is listed with regards to the ingredients and instructions required. There are also photos of each recipe in this book to give people ideas of how these foods are to look as they are finished.

All recipes are designed to be made as quickly as possible. These recipes can be prepared in 45 minutes or less and are good for multiple servings. All the items listed here are designed to be enjoyable for all sorts of people thanks to how they contain rich and easy to taste flavors.

# Contents

# Introduction

The Paleo diet has become one of the more interesting diets for people to follow with regards to keeping their bodies intact. It is a diet that's also known as the caveman diet.

The concept of the Paleo diet involves consuming foods that were based off of a diet that was theoretically used by men in the Paleolithic Era. This is a period of time that is more than 10,000 years in the past.

The concept of this diet is with the belief that by eating a diet without the artificial and processed ingredients of today's food, a person can lose weight and build muscle.

The Paleo diet requires plenty of proteins and fewer carbohydrates to help you stay strong and to build mass. It also entails plenty of fresh fruits and vegetables.

All of the recipes that you will read about in this book include all sorts of options dedicated to helping your body feel its best. In fact, these recipes are amazingly easy to prepare. You'll learn about all sorts of recipes in this guide including a few options that you can prepare in thirty minutes or less.

# Breakfast

## *Horseradish Scrambled Eggs with Bacon*

This is a recipe that can be prepared with raw bacon that has been mixed directly into the eggs. Try to trim off the excess fat materials from the bacon before cooking for the best results.

30 minutes

Serves 2

**Ingredients**

6 eggs

4 raw bacon slices

1 teaspoon of horseradish

**Instructions**

Heat a skillet over medium heat and slice up the bacon into a series of small bits.

Mix the eggs with horseradish as the bacon is cooking up.

Move the bacon out of the skillet when it is cooked and crisp. Don't forget to remove the grease.

Pour the eggs and horseradish into the skillet and cook until they are fully scrambled. Add all the bacon bits afterwards and mix them in before serving.

## *Almond Butter Pancakes*

Almond butter is recommended for the Paleo diet instead of traditional butter as it is made from the almond plant. It also has more fiber and calcium than butter.

30 minutes

Serves 2-4

**Ingredients**

3 eggs

3 bananas

1/4 cup of almond butter

1 tablespoon of coconut oil

**Instructions**

Mix the eggs and bananas together; the bananas do not have to be cut up but you can mash them as needed.

Add the almond butter into the mixture and stir it in.

Heat the coconut oil in a pan and move your pancake batter into the pan.

Cook on each side until the pancakes are fully browned; this can take 3 to 5 minutes per side but it all depends on how intense the heat is.

This can be garnished with all sorts of fruits like apples (see the picture above).

## *Spinach and Avocado Omelet*

Spinach is highly recommended in the Paleo diet as it includes plenty of fiber.

40 minutes

Serves 2-3

**Ingredients**

4 eggs

1 avocado

1 cup of chopped spinach

1 teaspoon of basil

1 teaspoon of olive oil

**Instructions**

Whisk the eggs while you heat the oil in a skillet. Add the eggs when they are fully mixed.

Add the spinach onto the eggs when the eggs are close to being fully cooked. Sprinkle this with basil and fold it in half.

Reduce the heat and cover and simmer for about a minute.

Add sliced avocado to the plate as a garnish.

## *Steak and Eggs*

Steak and eggs is a traditional Paleo meal that doesn't take as long to make as you might expect.

20 minutes

Serves 2

**Ingredients**

1 large steak; be sure to keep it refrigerated instead of frozen before using

2 eggs

2-3 tablespoons of almond butter

**Instructions**

Heat a pan at a medium-high level and add 2 tablespoons of almond butter.

Cook the steak on the pan until it reaches an appropriate level; it generally takes 3 to 5 minutes per side to cook it to a medium well level.

Remove the steak and turn the heat to a medium-low level. Add the remaining almond butter at this point.

Heat the eggs in the pan and cook until everything is grilled up.

You can add the eggs to the side of the steak or you can top the steak with eggs.

Note: Paprika, salt and pepper may also be added as a flavoring if desired.

## Green Eggs

Yes, green eggs do exist. This is a great way to get your vegetables in the morning.

25 minutes

Serves 2-4

**Ingredients**

4 eggs

4 kale leaves

A small bit of salt for taste

1/2 a tablespoon of coconut oil

**Instructions**

Mix your eggs, kale leaves and salt in a blender or processor. Everything should be smooth as it blends in.

Heat the coconut oil in a large pan at medium heat and add the mixture into it. Cook for a bit and then scramble the ingredients.

This can be cooked to your preference; it often takes 10 minutes for it to come out right.

# Lunch

## *Fishy Caesar Salad*

Fish can provide your body with plenty of omega-3s. Salmon is strongly recommended and will be used in this recipe but most other kinds of fish can be used too.

30 minutes

Serves 4

**Ingredients**

4 6-ounce skin-on fish filets, preferably salmon

2 chopped romaine lettuce heads

1/4 cup diced red onion

2 teaspoons of olive oil

1 garlic clove

1 teaspoon of mustard seed

1 teaspoon of lemon juice

**Instructions**

Brush the fish filets with olive oil and heat in an oven on broil for about 15 minutes.

Mix the lettuce and onion and add the mustard seeds, lemon juice and garlic.

Combine all items and serve with the fish filets after they have been fully cooked. You can add the fish filets on top of each serving but it's a good idea to cut them up.

## *Quick Chicken Salad with Vinegar Mayonnaise*

The chicken salad is a staple of many Paleo diets thanks to its impressive versatility.

25 minutes

Serves 2

**Ingredients**

1 cup of diced chicken

1/2 cup of diced red bell pepper

2 thin scallions

1 cup cherry tomatoes

1 chopped artichoke heart

1 package of spinach leaves (as seen above) or lettuce leaves

2 egg yolks

1 tablespoon of vinegar

1 tablespoon of lemon juice

2/3 cup of olive oil

**Instructions**

Mix the egg yolks, vinegar and lemon juice together.

Add about half your olive oil and then blend everything again. Add the other half afterwards and do the same.

Mix the dressing with the other ingredients listed above. You can add the dressing on top like in the sample seen above or you can immerse the other ingredients in with it. Be sure to keep everything except the cherry tomatoes diced as well as possible.

## Chicken and Avocado Soup

The healthy fats that come with the avocado make this an ideal product for soup.

30 minutes

Serves 4

**Ingredients**

6 cups of chicken stock

1 pound boneless chicken breast

1 diced avocado

4 scallions

1 garlic clove

**Instructions**

Add the chicken stock to a pot and heat at a medium-high level.

Slice the chicken and avocado into pieces.

Cut up the scallions by separating the green parts from the white.

Add the chicken and white scallion parts and stir.

Add the garlic and turn to a simmer for 10 minutes.

Mix the avocado and green scallion parts into the soup after it is finished.

## *Coconut Stir-Fry*

This recipe mixes chicken and broccoli in a warm stir-fry with curry powder.

25 minutes

Serves 2-4

### Ingredients

1 pound of sliced boneless chicken breast

2 cups of broccoli

1 can of coconut milk

1 cup of sliced mushrooms

1 1/2 teaspoons of curry powder

1 cup of spinach leaves

### Instructions

Mix the coconut milk and curry powder while you stir-fry the chicken in a large wok.

Remove the chicken after it is cooked; it should take about 5 to 8 minutes for it to be cooked.

Add broccoli into the stir-fry and cook for 3 minutes.

Add the chicken, spinach leaves, mushrooms, curry, and coconut milk in and cook for about 3 to 5 minutes or until the spinach is wilted.

You can add coconut flakes if desired.

## *Cilantro Pork Stir-Fry*

Pork is a healthy kind of meat to enjoy on the Paleo diet but it works particularly well when you add greens to it.

30 minutes

Serves 2-4

**Ingredients**

1 pound of sliced pork

1 cup of chopped cilantro leaves

2 sliced onions

1 sliced green pepper

1/4 cup of olive oil

**Instructions**

Stir-fry your pork in a wok at medium-high heat for about 5 to 8 minutes.

Add the onions into the wok and stir-fry for 3 more minutes.

Add the pepper and mix for 3 more minutes.

Mix the cilantro leaves with olive oil and cook in the wok for another minute. Be sure to mix everything so the flavors can mix in well.

## *Fennel Apple Soup*

The interesting thing about apples is that they can be made into its own soup with fennel bulbs.

30 minutes

Serves 4

**Ingredients**

2 apples peeled and cored

1 onion

2 fennel bulbs with the stems removed

1 quart of chicken stock

2 tablespoons of olive oil

**Instructions**

Heat the olive oil in a pot and sauté the onion over it for about 10 minutes.

Add the apples and fennel and cook for 5 to 10 minutes.

Add in the chicken stock and puree in a blender.

This may be reheated for about 2 to 3 minutes after you blend it.

## Zucchini Noodle Soup

While noodle soup can be great, there are too many preservatives in canned soup. You can make your own unique noodle soup on your own.

30 minutes

Serves 4

**Ingredients**

1 quart of chicken stock

1 zucchini

1 diced carrot

1 diced celery stalk

**Instructions**

Boil the chicken stock and then simmer.

Cut the zucchini with a julienne slicer to create a series of noodles. These should be durable thanks to the hard inside body of a raw zucchini.

Cook the carrots and celery for 10 to 20 minutes in the chicken stock.

Add the zucchini noodles and cook for about 5 more minutes.

# Dinner

## Pork Chops with Apples and Onions

Pork chops are great on their own but it's a good idea to add some additional ingredients as needed.

30 minutes

Serves 4

**Ingredients**

4 pork chops

3 tablespoons of coconut oil

2 large sliced onions

4 sliced apples

**Instructions**

Heat a pan over medium-high heat and melt 2 tablespoons of coconut oil in it. Add the pork chops and fry for five minutes on each side.

Turn the heat down by a bit and add the rest of the oil plus the apples and onions. Cook for 4 minutes so everything is browned and ready.

Serve the apples and onions on top of the pork chops.

## *Sausages with Parsnip Mash*

While sausages and potatoes are great, parsnip mash is a more appropriate Paleo diet substitute.

40 minutes

Serves 4-6

**Ingredients**

12 pork sausages

2 minced garlic cloves

2 pounds of chopped parsnip

5 tablespoons of coconut butter

1/2 cup of sliced red onions

1/2 cup of coconut milk

**Instructions**

Boil the parsnip for 15 minutes. As you do this, you can heat a skillet over medium heat and cook your sausages for about 15 minutes. Be sure to turn them on occasion.

After the parsnip is boiled, add half your coconut butter and add the coconut milk to it and mash all items up properly.

After the sausages are ready, remove them and cook the red onions for about 3 to 5 minutes. You can add garlic to them at this point.

All items can be served together. This may be served with vegetables on the side like the tomato in the picture above.

## *Baked Salmon and Asparagus*

A majority of the time spent making this recipe will involve preparing the recipe as the oven preheats; fortunately, the preparation should take about as much time as it will for the oven to heat up.

30 minutes

Serves 4

**Ingredients**

4 salmon filets

4 teaspoons of dill

4 tablespoons of coconut oil

16 sprigs of asparagus

**Instructions**

Heat your oven to 500 degrees and align your salmon onto aluminum foil.

Add one teaspoon of dill and one tablespoon of coconut oil on each filet.

Add the asparagus to the mixture while wrapping them in little pockets inside the aluminum foil so they will not become too hot.

Bake for 10 minutes for each inch of thickness in your salmon; in short, you might have to spend 15 or 20 minutes cooking this.

## Deviled Chicken

Chicken is known to be a good source of protein while on the Paleo diet. This recipe entails a way to create your own natural coating.

35 minutes

Serves 4

**Ingredients**

4 chicken legs and leg quarters

1 teaspoon of curry powder

1 teaspoon of cayenne powder

1 teaspoon of dry mustard

4 tablespoons of olive oil

1/2 cup of almond meal

**Instructions**

Cut the drumsticks away from the thighs and combine the almond meal with the seasonings.

Add olive oil to each drumstick and the roll into the almond meal mixture.

Bake at 350 degrees for around 25 minutes.

## *Paleo Fish Sticks*

Why buy processed fish sticks when you can make your own with real fish?

30 minutes

Serves 4

**Ingredients**

1 pound of white fish; this can include tilapia or cod

2 eggs

1 cup of almond flour

1/4 cup of olive oil

**Instructions**

Cut up your fish filets into a series of rolls that should be about one inch wide and three to five inches long. Remove all bones as needed.

Whisk two eggs and dip the sticks you created in the eggs.

Roll the sticks into the almond flour.

Add the olive oil onto a large skillet at medium-high heat.

Place the sticks onto the skillet and grill for about 10 minutes while turning the sticks over on occasion.

## *Salmon Burger Patties*

This is a recipe that can be served with buns if desired but it's best to avoid them if you want to stick to the Paleo diet. Besides, the salmon flavor is great on its own.

30 minutes

Serves 4-6

**Ingredients**

1 pound of salmon

1 tablespoon of sesame oil

1/4 cup of chopped red onions

1/4 cup of scallions

1/2 tablespoon of coconut oil

1 tablespoon of coconut flour (optional)

1 tablespoon of vinegar

**Instructions**

Cut the salmon into a series of two to four inch patties and mix with vinegar, sesame oil, onions and scallions.

You can add coconut flour onto the salmon patties if desired; this can be used as a coating.

Heat the coconut oil over a skillet at medium-high heat and cook all patties for about 10 minutes, flipping them midway through.

# Dessert

## *Peppermint Patties*

These are made to be more organic versions of the famous candies.

40 minutes

Serves 4-6

**Ingredients**

1 cup of chocolate chunks

1/2 cup of coconut oil

1/4 cup of honey

1/2 teaspoon of peppermint oil

**Instructions**

Mix the coconut oil, honey and peppermint oil and smash the oil clumps as they are formed. You need to make this as smooth as possible.

Freeze for about 15 to 20 minutes.

Melt the chocolate over medium heat as the first mixture is being frozen.

Scoop the oil and honey mixture out and flatten a series of balls into patties.

Dip all the patties into the chocolate and place them on a spot to harden. It can take about 10 minutes for them all to harden up.

## Paleo Fruitcake

This recipe requires almond flour, an organic alternative to traditional gluten-based flour.

40 minutes

Serves 4-6

**Ingredients**

1 cup of almond flour

1/4 teaspoon of baking soda

1/4 cup of chopped dates

1/4 cup of raisins

1/4 cup of cherries

1/2 cup of dried walnuts

1/2 cup of dried almonds

2 eggs

1 tablespoon of coconut oil

1/2 tablespoon of vanilla extract

**Instructions**

Combine the flour and baking soda and then stir in the fruits and nuts.

Mix the eggs, oil and vanilla together.

Mix all items into a fruitcake loaf pan.

Bake at 350 degrees for 30 minutes.

You can add additional dried almonds on the top of the batter before baking to add a cover if desired (see the picture above for an example).

## *Paleo Brownies*

You can also make brownies with almond flour to match up with your Paleo diet needs.

40 minutes

Serves 6-8

**Ingredients**

1 cup of almond flour

1/4 teaspoon of baking soda

4 ounces of chocolate

3 eggs

1/2 cup of coconut oil

1/2 teaspoon of vanilla

**Instructions**

Mix the almond flour and baking soda together.

Add the chocolate into the mixture and blend in a food processor.

Mix in the eggs and finally the coconut oil and vanilla.

Add to a baking pan and bake at 350 degrees for 20 to 24 minutes.

# Appetizers

## *Tropical Trail Mix*

It's easy to heat up almonds and coconuts to mix in with different foods.

20 minutes

Serves 4

**Ingredients**

2 cups of sliced almonds

1 cup of whole almonds

1 cup of coconut flakes

1 cup of macadamia nuts

1 cup of pumpkin seeds

1 cup raisins

1 cup chopped dates

**Instructions**

Cook the sliced almonds, dates and coconut flakes in a skillet over medium heat for 6 to 8 minutes or until everything is toasted. Let it cool for about 5 minutes afterwards.

Mix in the heated materials with the other ingredients. Break the macadamia nuts into pieces if desired. The whole almonds should not be cut up unless you feel like it.

## Steak Bites

These are simple finger foots that fit in well for any party.

25 minutes

Serves 4-6

**Ingredients**

1 pound of sirloin steak

2 tablespoons of coconut oil

Salt and pepper for flavor

**Instructions**

Cut up the sirloin steak and trim off any fatty deposits. Make them less than one inch in size each.

Heat your skillet with coconut oil at medium high heat.

Cook the meat and keep it steady for about 45 to 60 seconds before turning it over. Be sure to repeat this for about 10 to 15 minutes or until the steak is fully cooked.

Add salt and pepper for flavoring midway through.

## Banana Chips

You can make your own banana chips by baking them over a light amount of heat.

35 minutes

Serves 2

**Ingredients**

1 large sliced banana

1 tablespoon of orange juice; be sure this is squeezed from fresh oranges

**Instructions**

Slice up your banana and squeeze your orange juice on top. Make sure everything is covered as evenly as possible.

Cook for 30 minutes at 200 degrees Fahrenheit.

The banana chips will be a little chewier than what you might be used to but they will be completely fresh.

## Carrot Fries

You shouldn't be eating potatoes during the Paleo diet but that doesn't mean you can't enjoy fries.

30 minutes

Serves 4

### Ingredients

1 1/2 pounds of carrots

2 tablespoons of olive oil

1/2 teaspoon of salt

2 teaspoons of rosemary

### Instructions

Cut and peel your carrots and make them into a series of long fries. You can get about six to eight fries for each carrot you use.

Mix the carrots with the oil, rosemary and salt. Make sure everything is evenly covered.

Bake the carrots at 425 degrees for 20 minutes.

These can be served hot if desired.

6604628R10019

Printed in Great Britain
by Amazon.co.uk, Ltd.,
Marston Gate.